Captain Tollemache's Journal Of The Proceedings Of H. M. S. Scorpion, June 21, 1775 To September 18, 1775

John Tollemache

In the interest of creating a more extensive selection of rare historical book reprints, we have chosen to reproduce this title even though it may possibly have occasional imperfections such as missing and blurred pages, missing text, poor pictures, markings, dark backgrounds and other reproduction issues beyond our control. Because this work is culturally important, we have made it available as a part of our commitment to protecting, preserving and promoting the world's literature. Thank you for your understanding.

CAPTAIN TOLLEMACHE'S
JOURNAL
OF THE
PROCEEDINGS
OF
H. M. S. SCORPION
June 21, 1775 -- September 18, 1775

EDITED BY
A. S. SALLEY, JR.
Secretary of the Historical Commission
of South Carolina

PRINTED FOR THE COMMISSION
By The State Company
Columbia, S. C.
1919

INTRODUCTION.

The journal here printed is of interest to South Carolinians because the *Scorpion* brought Lord William Campbell to South Carolina in 1775, and almost immediately became involved in the proceedings which preceded the breaking out of hostilities between Great Britain and the American provinces. *The South-Carolina Gazette; And Country Journal* for May 30, 1775, announced:

On Friday last arrived here the Brig Rebecca, Capt. Sanders, who informs us, the Scorpion Man of War was on the 23d. of last Month at Madeira, on board of which, according to the latest advices, Lord William Campbell was to embark for this Province, so that his arrival may be hourly expected.

The same paper for Tuesday, June 20, 1775, published the following:

On Saturday evening last his excellency the Right Hon. Lord William Campbell, Gov. &c. of this Province, with his Lady and family arrived in the Scorpion Man of War from England.

This journal is in the British Public Records Office under Admiralty, Captains Logs, Volume 872.

A Journal of the Proceedings of His Majesty's
Sloop Scorpion between 21st. June and 18th. Septr. 1775
kept by the Honble Jno. Tollemache.

Week Days.	Mo. Days	Winds	Course	Distce.	Lattd. in	Longd. made	Bearings & Distce: at Noon
June 1775 Wednesdy—	21	East	"	"	"	"	Moor'd in Charles Town Harbour So- Carolina.
Thursdy—	22	Do.	"	"	"	"	
Friday	23	Do.	"	"	"	"	
Saturdy:	24	S S E S W W S W	"	"	"	"	
Sunday	25	West S W	"	"	"	"	
Mondy.	26	Do.	"	"	"	"	Moor'd in Rebellion Road. Fort Johnson S W Sullivans Island E½N
Tuesday	27	S. W	"	"	"	"	
Wednesdy-	28	Do.	"	"	"	"	
Thursdy.	29	S W W N W E S E	"	"	"	"	
Friday	30	So-erly	"	"	"	"	
July Saturday	1	S W	"	"	"	"	
Sunday	2	Do.	"	"	"	"	
Mondy.	3	S W	"	"	"	"	
Tuesdy.	4	S W W S W W B S	"	"	"	"	At Single Anchor off Charles Town Bar.[1]

[1] "This Day the Scorpion Man of War, sailed for Cape Fear."—*The South-Carolina Gazette; And Country Journal*, Tuesday, July 4, 1775.
"On Tuesday last his Majestys sloop Scorpion, commanded by Hon. Capt. Tollemache sailed for Boston."—*The South-Carolina and American General Gazette*, Friday, July 7, 1775.

Remarks &c.

Fresh Breez⁸ and Clear, sent a Petty Officer and two Men to Hobcaw to compleat the Watering. Left the Duty on Shore Andw. Herron.

Do: W. Recd. Water and Fresh Beef, left the Duty on Shore Jams. Oakes Marine

D: W. Empd: Watering. Left the Duty on Shore Josh: Payne Marine.

D: W. Stay'd the Masts and set the Rigging up, Pay'd the Ships sides with Tar Empd: Watering. Recd: Provisions, Punish'd Wm. Tompkins Marine with 12 Lashes for Disobedience of Orders.

Do: W. Recd: on board Rum for the Ships Company. Empd. Watering left the Boat on Duty Jno. Laws and Richd: Ellis Seaman made a Signal for a Pilot, the Pilot came on board.

Do: W. P. M. Recd: on board Wood and Water, at 5 A M Unmoor'd & hove Short on the Bt. Bower at 8 Weigh'd and Came to Sail at ½ past 9 came too with the Bt Bower in Rebellion Road at 10 Moor'd Ship.

Do: W. Heel'd Ship and Bootop'd both Sides.

First and Middle parts Fresh Gales, and Squally with Thunder Lightning and Rain, Latter Fresh Breezs. and fair Empd. Watering Dry'd Sail. Left the Duty on Shore Isaac Edwards Marine and Wm. Watts Cooper.

First part Fresh Gales and Squalles with Thunder Lightning and Rain Middle and latter Fresh Gales and fair, P. M. Empd. Watering A M Dry'd Sails the Pilot came on bd: and took Charge of the Ship. Recd: Fresh Beef. Left the Boat on Duty Felix Mc.Ginnes

Fresh Breezs. and Cloudy Empd: Occasionally Recd: Water.

Do. W. Empd: as before Recd. Fresh Beef

First part Fresh Breezs. and hazey, Middle Squles. with Thunder Lightg. & Rain, latter Fresh Breezs. & fair AM Dry'd Sails.

Fresh Breezs. and fair Dry'd Sails Empd: Preparing for Sea.

First part Mode with Rain Middle and latter Do. and fair at 3 AM Unmoor'd and hove Shore on the Bt. Bower at 6 Weigh'd and came to Sail ½ past 9 came too off Charles Town Bar. in ½ less 7 fathm. Charles Town Light house W B N 4 or 5 Miles.

Week Days	Mo. Days	Winds	Course.	Distce:	Lattd. in	Longd: made	Bearings & Distce: at Noon
July 17 Wednesdy.	5[1]	S B W S W B S	"	"	"	"	Cape Fear N N E 12 or 13 Leags.
Thursdy	6	S W B S S W B W S W	"	"	"	"	At Single Anchor of Cape Fear Bar.
Friday	7[2]	S W W N N E	"	"	"	"	
Saturdy	8	E B N N E	"	"	"	"	
Sunday	9	E B N N E	So. 32 E	33ms	33.22 No.	00.21 E	Cape Fear No. 32 W 11 Leags:
Monday	10	Varble	No: 71 E	8	33.25 N.	00.30 E.	Do. N W 12 Leags.
Tuesdy.	11	Do:	No: 83 W.	31	33.29 N.	00.10 W.	Do: No: 00.22 E 7 Leags:
Wednesdy	12	Do:	So. 85 E.	56	33.33 N.	00.49 E.	Do: No: 67 W. 13 Leags:
Thursdy.	13	Varble	No. 66 E	134ms	34.27 N	3.15 E.	Cape Fear So. 77 E. 55 Leags.
Friday	14	W. B N N W S W	N. 35 E	106	35.54 N.	4.30 Et	Cape Hatteras So. 69 30 E. 37 Leags.
Saturdy	15	Varble	No. 38 E.	72	36.25 N.	4.54 E.	Do. So. 65 E. 55 Leagues.

[1] "I have the honor to inform your Lordship that I received your several Dispatches by the Sandwich Packet yesterday, through the hands of Captain Tolemache Commander of His Majesty's Ship *Scorpion*, who has touched here on his way from Charles Town to Boston, for the sole purpose of delivering them."—Extract from a letter from Governor Martin, of North Carolina, to Lord Dartmouth, dated Fort Johnston, July 6, 1775, published in *The Colonial Records of North Carolina*, Volume X, pp. 69-71.

[2] "I have engaged Mr Alexr Schaw whom I have now the honor to introduce to your Lordship to charge himself with this Letter and my Dispatch No. 34." . . . . "Mr Schaw My Lord is an officer in the Customs in the Island of St. Christophers" . . . . "and was preparing to return to it, when Captain Tollemache's

Remarks &c.

Fresh Breez^s. and hazey at 7 PM Weigh'd and came to Sail, kept Sounding

First and Middle parts Fresh Breez^s. and Clouds latter Mode: at 3 PM saw the Land from N W B N to N E b N ½ past 4 PM came too with the B^c Br. in 7 fa^m. Water Veer'd away to ½ a Cable. Cape Fear E b N ½ N 5 or 6 Miles Veer'd to a whole Cable.

First part Mode: & Cloudy. Middle Fresh Breez^s. with Thunder and Lightning latter Fresh Gales and Cloudy Emp^d. Occasionally, Supply His Maj. Sloop Cruizer with 1 Puncheon of Beef 1 4^{ins} Hawser 24 Hammocks, 4½ Barrels of Powder & some Rope, Rec^d. from her 2 old Cables one of 94 & the other of 46 fa^{ms}. a 6^{ins} Hawser of 76 fa^{ms}.

Fresh Breez^s. and Clear Emp^d: Occasionally.

Mod. Breez^s. and fair. PM Spared to Fort Johnson 3½ Barrels of Powder, at 12 hove Short, Weig'd and Came to Sail Pilot still on board.

First part Squally with Rain, Middle and Latter Light Breez^s. & fair PM. Sounded, Jack'd Ship Occas^{ly}, at 9 AM saw a Sail in the NW Quarter, Wore & gave Chace Fir'd two 6 Pounders Shotted at the Chace.

First and Middle parts Mod^e & Clear, latter Squally with Rain, at 3 PM Haul'd our Wind to the No.ward Sounded, & K^d. Ship Occas^{ly}. in Stays Carried away the Mⁿ. Tops^l. Yard Emp^d: getting another up at 2 AM got the Yard across and bent the Sail.

Mod^e and Hazey kept the Lead going & K^d. Occas^{ly}. at 6 PM. Came too with the B^t Bow^r. Veer'd away to ½ a Cable. Hoist'd the Boat out & try'd the Current, found it to set E N E 2½ Miles pr. hour. at 1 AM Weigh'd & came to Sail, the Lead Continually going.

First part Mode. & Cloudy. Middle & latter Fresh Breez^s. and Clear PM Sounded no Ground, at 10 AM Exercis'd Great Guns & Small Arms & fir'd at a Mark.

First part Fresh Breez^s. and hazey, Middle Squally with Thunder, Light^g & Rain, latter part Mod^e & hazey. Sounded no Ground. Punish'd W^m. Escott Seaman with 12 Lashes for Theft.

First and Middle parts Mod^e. & Clear, latter Mod^e. OCloudy at ½ past 5 PM spoke a Sloop from Philadelphia bound to Providence. Sailmakers Emp^d. repairing the Jibb.

arrival presented me with so fair an occasion to employ him advantageously for His Majesty's Service" .... "nothing remained but that I should engage Capt. Tollemache to stay 48 hours beyond the time he had appointed for his departure for my Dispatches and Mr Schaw's necessary preparation, which that officer most politely agreed at my request to do."—Ibid.
"P: S: This will be delivered to you by my Brother who has just stole up from the Sound to bid me farewell; he has not an hour to stay, he goes home with dispatches from the Governo^r" .... "Thank God my Brother got safe on Board the King's Ship and Sailed with 'ap^t. Tallmash in his Friget that same afternoon for England".—From a letter written from Wilmington at this time by Miss Jen. Schaw, and now in possession of Mr. Vere L. Oliver, of Whitmore Lodge, Sunninghill, England.

Week Days	Mo-Days	Winds	Course	Distce.	Lattd. in	Longd. made	Bearings & Distce: at Noon
July 17 Sunday	75 16	W S W N W N B E	No 43 Et	55	37.05 N	5.41 E	St. Georges Shoals No. 20 E 94 Leags.
Monday	17	Var ble	No 10 Et.	31	37.35 N	5.48 E	Nantucket Shoals No. 43 E. 61 Leags.
Tuesday	18	S E NWBW S W	No 44 Et	52	38.12 N	6.33 E	Do. No. 43 Et. 45 Leags.
Wednesdy.	19	S W No W N W	No. 49 Et.	68	39.01 N	7.44 E	Do. No. 36 Et. 20 Leagues
Thursdy.	20	Varble	No. 44. 30 E	67	39.48	8.44 E	So. End of St. Georges Bank. No. 20 Et. 48 Leags:
Friday	21	Varble	No. 50 Et.	47	40.18 N	9.17 Et.	So. End of St. Georges Bank No. N Et 30 Leags.
Saturday	22	NEBE N E N NE	No. 17 W	54	41.07 N	9.57 Et.	St. Georges Shoals No. 20 W 14 Leags:
Sunday	23	Varble	N. 20 W	43	41.47 N	9.53 Et.	St. Georges Bank So. 80 W. 4 or 5 Leags.

Remarks &c.

First part Fresh Breezs. and Cloudy. Middle Squalles with Rain Thunder & Lightning, latter light Airs & Cloudy at 5 AM 1st. Rf. Topsails Kd & Wore Ship.

First part Calm & Cloudy, Middle light Breezs. and Cloudy, latter Mode. with Rain, at 2 PM Air'd the Sails, found holes in the Courses eat by the Mice at ½ past 5 try'd the Current found it set NE ½ mile Pr- hour at 6 hoisted in the Boat and made Sail, at 8 taken a back

---

First and latter parts Mode. Breezs. with Rain, Middle Light Breezes & Cloudy, latter Mode. & fair PM a large Swell from the SW, at 7 Shorten'd sail hove to and Sounded 140 fathms. no Ground. Wore and made Sail at 5 AM two Sail in Sight, Split the Fore T. Ge. Sails. Empd. Repairing Do., at Noon Spoke a Ship from Newry to Philadelphia.

First and Middle parts Light Breezs. & fair, latter Mode. & Cloudy, at 4 PM two Sail in Sight at 11 Shorten'd Sail hove to and Sound'd no Ground 100 fathms., Wore and made Sail at 6 saw a Sail to the Wt.ward.

First part Fresh Gales and heavy Squalls with Rain. Middle Mode. and Hazey with Rain, latter Squally with Rain, at 2 PM Shorten'd Sail and hove to Spoke a Vessell from Liverpool, ½ past Spoke a Ship from Glasgow, at 5 PM Carried away the Starbd: Fore & Mn. Topmast, Steering Sail Booms. Close Reeft the Topsails Struck. T. Gt. Masts and Yards.

First and latter part Fresh Gales and Squally with Rain Middle Mode. & hazey with Rain, Spoke 2 Vessels from England. at 5 PM Carried away the Starbd. Fore & Main Topmt. Steering sail Booms, Close Reeft Topsails and T. Gallt. masts Struck.

First part Mode. & Cloudy with Squalls Middle & latter Calm at 1 PM hove to, Spoke a Schooner from Connecticut at 3 Kd. & set Single Rf. T. Sails at 8 up T. Gallt. Yards Sounded 110 fams. no Ground, saw a Sail to the Wt.ward.

Light Airs and Clear, at 3 PM saw a Sail in the NW Quarter ½ past 6 hove to & spoke His Majesty's Ship Glasgow from Boston on a Cruize, at 8 made Sail, at 5 AM saw a Sail in the NW Quartr. ½ past hove to Spoke a Snow from Piscataway to Tobago. Wore and made Sail.

Week Days	Mo. Days	Winds	Course	Distce.	Lattd. in	Longd. made	Bearings & Distce. at Noon
July 17 Monday	75 24	SWBS SW SWBW	No. 61 W	82	42.26 N	9.43 Et	Boston Lighthouse W. 52 Leags:
Tuesday	25	Varble	No. 89 W	36	42.25 N	9.03 Et	Do. West 40 Leags.
Wednesdy.	26	W SW South	No. 68 W	18	43.32 N	8.38 Et.	Do. No. 86 W. 32 Leags:
Thursdy.	27	S.BW	"	"	"	"	Not Seeing the Land imagine the Current has set us to the Et. Wd.
Friday	28	SBW½W SBW South SBW	"	"	"	"	
Saturdy.	29	SSW W SW SSW	"	"	"	"	Moor'd in Boston Harbr: Castle William SE½S Long Wharfe WNW
Sundy.	30	W NW	"	"	"	"	
Mondy.	31	W SW WSW	"	"	"	"	

Remarks, &c.

First part mode. & fair. Middle Fresh Gales and Cloudy, latter Fresh Gales and Squally with Rain. Sounded every hour no Ground out 2d Rfs., at noon hove to spoke a Brig from Boston to London.

First part Fresh Breezs. and Foggy Wt., Middle Mode. & Clear. Latter light Airs & fair, at 12 Sounded 130 fams. no Ground at 2 A. M. Kd: Ship at 8 Sounded 130 fams. brown Sand.

First part Light Airs & fair. Middle Do. with a thick Fog. Latter light Airs & hazey at 2 P. M. saw a Sail to the W.ward at 5 Sounded soft muddy Ground. Set T. Gallt. Sails out 1st Reefs.

First and Middle parts Light Breezs. & foggy, with Lightning & Rain latter mode. & fair at 8 P M hove to & Sounded 110 fams. soft Muddy Ground.

First & Middle parts Light Breez*. and Hazey with Rain, latter mod*. and fair. Sounded 55 fam. hard Ground at 4 P M saw the Land from WNW to NWBN ½ past 11 Came to with the Bt. Bower in 23 fam., fir'd a Gun & made a Signal for a Pilot at 12 Repeated the Signal, at 6 A M hove in to ⅛ of a Cable Fir'd a Gun for a Pilot at 8 Weigh'd & came to Sail at 10 Came onbd. a Pilot.

First part Light Breez* and hazey with Rain, latter part mod*. & fair, P M Empd. working into Nantasket Bay in Company with His Maj. Ships Merlin & Falcon, at 8 Came to in Boston Harbour with the Bt. Bower in 5 fam. water, Veer'd to ½ a Cable found riding here His Majs. Ships the Preston Vice Adml. Graves and Sommerset with a large Fleet of Transports, at 5 AM Saluted Adml. Graves with 13 Guns, Moor'd Ship with the Stream Anchor to the So.ward. Castle William SE ½ S. Long Wharfe WNW at 10 Punish'd Jas. Ryan for Drunkeness

First part Fresh Gales and Clear, Middle mode. & latter fresh Breezs. & fair, sent on shore the Empty Water Casks Recd: Water.

Do. W. Empd. Watering, at 8 sent a Boat with a party of Men, Man'd & Arm'd on a Secret Expedition, at 7 A M Weigh'd the Stearn Anchor at 9 Weighed & came to Sail, hove to made Sail Occasly.

Week Days	Mo: Days	Winds	Course	Distce.	Lattd: in	Longd. made	Bearings & Distce: at Noon
August 17 Tuesdy.	75 1	W.erly Calm SSE	"	"	"	"	Moor'd off the Lighthouse Point Alderton SSE ¾ E Lighthouse NNE ¼ E.
Wednesdy.	2	Do.	"	"	"	"	
Thursdy.	3	SE NNW	"	"	"	"	Moor'd in Boston Harbour.
Friday	4	WNW W.erly NW.	"	"	"	"	
Saturdy.	5	W.erly	"	"	"	"	
Sunday	6	Do.	"	"	"	"	Moor'd in Cambridge River.
Monday	7	ENE East	"	"	"	"	
Tuesdy.	8	ENE Calm W.erly	"	"	"	"	
Wednesdy.	9	WSW West	"	"	"	"	

Remarks &c.
Mode. Breezs. & fair ½ past 1 P M came to with the Bt. Br. in 5 fam. off the Lighthouse, Veer'd to ½ a Cable, at 4 Veer'd away & Moor'd a Cable each way with Springs on them, our Boat return'd with the Officer and Men at 9 fir'd 4 Shot at the Rebels on Shore at the Lighthouse, sent a Boat Man'd and Arm'd to watch their motions. People under Arms all night AM Emp^d: making Boarding Nettings &c.
D^o. W. Emp^d: as before AM sent the Boat on shore to Watch the motion of the Rebels, at 11 unmoor'd & hove Short on the Small B^r. Punished Geo. Payler Marine for Neglect of Duty
D^o. W. at 2 PM Weighed & came to Sail ½ past 5 came too with the Br. Bower in Boston Harbour Moor'd with the Stream Anchor, at 6 made the Sign^l. for a Pilot ½ past the Pilot came onb^d: at 7 Weigh'd & came to Sail Stood up the Harbour, at 9 Came to with the Bt. Bow^r. ½ past 10 AM Fir'd a Gun and made the Signal for Assistance. Came onb^d: Mr. Jas. Drew Lieut. Rec^d: his Commissⁿ: at 11 Weigh'd & Carried the Stream Anch^r. out, the Ship Sheering too near the Shore let go the Un^d. Bow^r. under foot Carried the Bt. Br. Anchor out to Windward.
Mode. & fair at 3 PM Weigh'd the Small B^r. & hove Short on the Bt Bower Fir'd a Gun and made a Signal for Assistance, Boats of the Fleet Emp^d. Carrying out Anchors & Warps, at 8 came too with the Bt. Br. off Charles Town at 4 Weigh'd and Warp'd abreast the Mouth of Cambridge River.
Mode. & Clear Veer'd away & Moor'd with the Stream Cable fast to the Ring of the Small B^r to Moor head & Stern AM Row'd Guard, Emp^d. Occas^{ly}.
D^o. W. Anchor'd here His Maj^s. Ship Fowey, Lashed Booms across the Cables to prevent being Boarded by the Rebels. Read the Articles of War &c.
D^o. W. with Rain, Emp^d. Watering, Punished Geo: Mortimer with 12 Lashes for Neglect of Duty.
Mode: & Clear, Rec^d. Spruce Beer. Punished W^m. Smallshanks with 12 Lashes for Disobedience of Orders. Rec^d. Boatswains & Carpenters Stores Emp^d. Watering.
Varble W. Carpenters making a New F. T. Sail. Yard Emp^d. making Nippers.

Week Days	Mo. Days	Winds	Course	Distce.	Lattd: in	Longd: made	Bearings & Distce. at Noon.
August 17 Thursdy.	75 10	SW SSW Calm	"	"	"	"	Moor'd in Cambridge River
Friday	11	East NE	"	"	"	"	Single Anchor off Charles Town
Saturdy.	12	Calm NW	"	"	"	"	
Sunday	13	W.erly	"	"	"	"	
Monday	14	NW	"	"	"	"	
Tuesday	15	SE W.erly	"	"	"	"	Moor'd in Boston Harbour Castle William SE ½ E Long Wharfe WSW
Wednesdy.	16	W.erly	"	"	"	"	
Thursdy.	17	W.erly	"	"	"	"	
Friday	18	Do.	"	"	"	"	
Saturdy	19	W.erly NE	"	"	"	"	
Sunday	20	W.erly	"	"	"	"	
Monday	21	SW	"	"	"	"	
Tuesdy.	22	SW W WNW	"	"	"	"	Moor'd in Nantasket Road
Wednesdy.	23	SBW South	East	81	42.30 N	1.49 E	St. Georges Bank So. 47 E 32 Leags.

Remarks, &c.

First and Middle parts Fresh Gales and Squally with Rain, latter Calm and Cloudy, Carpenters Emp^d. Fir'd a Six pound^r. Shott'd at the Rebels. Emp^d. Waters.

Mode. with Thunder & Lightning, AM Unmoor'd, Fir'd a Gun and made Signal for Assistance Weigh'd and Warp'd abreast of Charles Town.

First part Calm with Rain, Middle and latter Light Airs & Cloudy, at 2 PM came too with the B^t. B^r. in Boston Harb^r. Moor'd with the Stream Anch^r. found riding here the Preston, Somerset, Kings Fisher & Cancer.

Mode. & Cloudy, Rec^d. Provisions. Dry'd Sails.

Light Breez^s. & fair Emp^d. Watering. AM. Air'd the Spare Sails. Rec^d. Rum & Shingle Ballast.

D^o. W. Rec^d: Bread & Pease & Shingle Ballast Caulkers, Emp^d. on board.

D^o. W. Rec^d. Provisions & Boatswains Stores, Shipwrights & Caulkers. Emp^d. onboard.

Mode. & fair. Rec^d: Boatswain's Stores, got up a New Fore Tops^l. Yard, Kiel'd & Bootop'd Caulkers & Shipwrights Emp^d: onboard.

D^o. W. Artificiers as before Emp^d. Boarding Vessells, Punish'd Robt: Eames with 12 Lashes for Mutiny, Dry'd Sails.

D^o. W. Rec^d. on board Water, Emp^d. as before, AM Sailed hence His Maj^s. Ship Somerset.

D^o. W. Emp^d. Occasly. Dry'd Sails.

D^o. W. Emp^d. boarding Vessels AM getting Ready for Sea, at 10 a Pilot came onboard.

D^o. W. PM Unmoor'd ½ past 1 Weighed & Came to Sail at 7 Came too with the Best B^r. in Nantasket Road, Veer'd away & Moor'd with Springs on the Cables, Town of Nantasket S E B S Long Island N W B W, found Riding here His Maj^s. Sloop Merlin, Emp^d. Watering.

Fresh Gales & Squally at 3 PM Unmoor'd & hove Short on the B^t. B^r. ½ past 7 Weighed & came to Sail the Pallaser in Company, the Lighthouse W B N 3 miles at 11 in T Gall^t. Sails, at 3 AM Rft. Topsails at 4 saw a Sail on the Larb^d. Bow, hove to Spoke a Sloop for Nantucket, made Sail. Transport in Company.

Week Days.	Mo. Days.	Winds	Course	Distce.	Lattd: in	Longd: made.	Bearings & Distce. at Noon
August 17 Thursdy.	75 24	W S W W NE	E ¾ S	96	42.16 N	3.58 Et.	Do: So: 41 W 13 Leags:
Friday	25	Varble	So 73 E	27	42.08 N.	4.33 Et.	Charles Town So. 46 W 276 Leags.
Saturdy—	26	Do.	No. 8 W	29	42.34 N	66.08 W	Do. So. 45 W 281 Leags.
Sundy.	27	Do:	So. 8 W	95	42.20 N	66.11 W	Do. So. 45 W 278 Leags.
Monday	28	Varble	So. 69 Et.	42	42.10 N	65.19 W	Charles Town So. 48 W 284 Leags.
Tuesdy	29	South S B W	No. 87 Et.	53	42.13 N	64.08 W	Do. So. 50 W 299 Leags.
Wednesdy.	30	S S W S W S W B S	S E	48	41.39 N	63.34 W	Do. So. 53 W 301 Leags.
Thursdy	31	S W S S E S B E	So. 37 E	32	41.48 N	63.09 W.	Do. So. 55 W 304 Leags.
Septemr. Friday	1	Varble	So. 73 E	42	42.07 N.	62.17 W.	Do. So. 57 W 312 Leags.
Saturdy.	2	S W B W W S W S S W	So. 34 Et	56	40.21 N	61.30 W	Do. So. 63 W 339 Leags.

Remarks &c.

Fresh Gales and hazey at 4 AM Sounded 45 fa^m. Coarse brown Sand being Foggy lost Sight of the Transport at 11 hove to Fir'd Six 6 Poundrs. & 20 Musquets as Signals to her.

First part Mode. & Foggy Middle & latter Mode. & Clear at 2 PM saw the Transport at 6 joined Compy.

Mode. & fair at 3 PM Sounded 70 f^m. no Ground. Emp^d. Repairing the larger Cutter. Recv'd a New Tiller Rope. Transport in Compy.

First part Mode. & Clear Middle & latter Foggy at 2 PM hove too supplied the Transport with 10 Musquets & 10 Cartouch Boxes at 2 AM lost sight of her Tinckled the Bell & fir'd Musq^{ts}. which she Answer'd at 8 saw the Transport.

First and Middle parts light Airs & Foggy Latter Mode. & Clear, at 9 PM lost Sight of the Transport Fir'd Musquets and Tinckl'd the Bell which she Answ'd. at 1 AM Fir'd a 6 Pounder which the Transport Answ^d. at 8 saw a Sail in the SE Fir'd a 6 Pounder Shotted & brought her too, Hove too Main Tops^l. to the Mast a Ship from Londonderry for Rhode Island ½ past 10 K^d. & made Sail Transport in Compy.

First p^t. Mode. & Clear. Middle & latter light Airs & Foggy 5 PM saw a Sail in the NE, gave Chace at 6 left off Chace, at 3 AM lost Sight of the Transp^t. Tinckl'd the bell which she Answ^d. fir'd a 6 Pounder as p Signal to her.

Light Breez^s. & a thick Fog at 2 PM Transport fir'd a Gun Answ^d. D^o. at 4 saw the Transport at 10 Lightning in the NW.

First p^t. Light Airs & fair Middle Squally with Thunder Lightning & Rain latter Mod. & Cloudy at 1 AM in st.Rf. T. Sails at 7 out Reefs

---

First & Middle p^{ts}. Light Breez^s. & Cloudy latter Fresh Breez^s. & Clear at 2 PM K^d. at 10 AM in 1^s Rf. T. Sails Transport in Company.

Fresh Breez^s. & Squally with Rain at 4 PM out Rfs. at 12 Fir'd a Gun & K. as p. Sign^l. at 2 AM K^d. & fir'd a Gun at 6 Close Reeft T. Sails, Hand'd Fore & Miz^n. T. Sails Struck T. G. M^{ts}. & Yards. Transport in Company.

Week Days	Mo. Days	Winds	Course	Distce.	Lattd: in	Longd: made	Bearings & Distce. at Noon
Septembr. Sunday	1775 3	S W B W West W B S N E b N	South	64	39.18 N	61.30 W.	Do So. 65 W 308 Leags.
Monday	4	N E East South S S W	So. 22 Et.	61	38.22	61.01 W	Do. So. 68 W 310 Leags.
Tuesdy.	5	S W	So. 54 Et.	73	37.39 N	59.46 N	Charles Town So: 73 W 304 Leags.
Wednesdy.	6	S W S E S W B S W S W	No. 4 W.	48	38.16 N	59.51 N	Do. So. 69 W 327 Leags.
Thursdy.	7	Varble	So. 9 Et.	33	37.55 N	59.44 N	Do. So. 71 W 326 Leags.
Friday	8	Do.	No. 83 W.	44	38.00 N	60.40 W.	Do. So. 70 W. 312 Leags.
Saturdy.	9	W B S North N E B E	South	66	36.54 N.	60.40 W.	Do. So. 74 W. 307 Leags.
Sunday	10	Do.	No. 85 W	32	36.56 N.	61.20 W.	Do. S. 73 W 298 Leags:

Remarks &c.

First pt. Fresh Gales and Squally with Rain. Middle Mode. latter Light Airs & fair at 6 PM hove too Mn. Topse. to the Mast at 7 bore down to the Transport sett Close Rf. Topsails up T. G. Mts. & Yards at 10 out 2 Reefs at 2 AM saw a Sail to the Et.wd. made Sail and gave Chace, at 3 Sett Steering Sails ½ past Spoke the Chace a Sloop from Cape Cod, at 6 made Sail, Read Articles of War &c to the Ships Company.

First part Light Breezs. latter Fresh Breezs. & Clear at 6 PM saw a Sail to the So. wd. gave Chace, Fir'd 2 Shott at the Chace at 7 lost sight of her made Signl. & Kd. at 3 AM saw a Sail to the Et.ward gave Chace, at 7 left off Chace, Split the Jib. Sailmn. Empd. Repg. it in Compy. as before.

Fresh Breezs. & Cloudy at 1 PM in 2d. Reefs at 6 saw 3 Sail gave Chace at 8 left off Chace at 10 Handed Mizn. T. Sail at 4 AM saw a Sail to the Et.ward, made Sail and gave Chace, at 6 fir'd a Shot at the Chace. at 8 Hove too spoke a Sloop from Cape Fear in 1m. Rfs. and made Sail to the SE gave Chace fir'd a Shott at the Chace.

First pt. Fresh Gales and Cloudy with Squalls at 3 PM fir'd 2 Shot at the Chace at 6 fir'd 2 Shot at the Chace & brot. her too Hove too & Exam'd her a Brig from Sr. Cruze for Milford Haven at 8 made Sail at 2 AM in 2d. Rfs. at 8 Split the Jibb at 10 Close Reeft T. Sails Struck T. Gt. Yards & Masts. Transport in Company.

First pt Strong Gales and Cloudy Middle & Latter Mode. at 1 PM Handed F & Mizn. T. Sails at 4 set Do. at 7 up T. G. Masts out Reefs. Transport in Company.

First and Middle parts Mode. & hazey latter Squally with rain, in 2d Reefs. Transport in Company.

First and Middle parts Fresh Gales and Squally with Rain, latter Mode. & Clear, ½ past 3 PM Kd: in 3d. Reefs at 4 Handed Fore and Mizn. T. Sails at 9 Sett Fore & Mizn. T. Sails out Reefs at 5 AM Split Mn. T. Gallt. Sail Repaired Do. in Compy. as before.

Light Airs & Cloudy in Company as before.

Week Days	Mo. Days.	Winds	Course.	Distce.	Lattd. in	Longd: made	Bearings & Distce. at Noon
Septembr. Monday	1775 11	S W S B W S W B S	No. 84 W	65	37.03 N	62.37 W	Do. S. 71 W 271 Leags.
Tuesday	12	S S W W N W N W B N	So. 33 Et.	6	36.58	63.45 W	Do. So. 70 W 270 Leags.
Wednesdy.	13	N W.B N North	So. 38 W	90	35 41 N	64.29 W.	Do. So. 76 W 245 Leags.
Thursdy.	14	No. East	So. 30 W	72	34.39 N	65.45 W	Cape Fear So. 85 W 201 Leags.
Friday	15	East S E	So. 39 W	102	33.20 N.	66.58 W	Do. No. 88 W 184 Leags.
Saturdy.	16	S E B E E b S East	So. 44 W	87	32.28	"	Do. No. 80.33 166 Leags.
Sunday	17	East E B S E S E	"	"	"	"	St. David's Head SSW 4 or 5 Miles.
Monday	18	East E S E	"	"	"	62.41 W	Moor'd in St. Georges Harbour Island of Bermuda[1]

[1] The *Scorpion* appears to have continued cruising off the east coast of North America from Boston to the West Indies. *The South-Carolina Gazette; And Country Journal* for December 2, 1775, says:

"On Wednesday of last week, arrived here from Cape-Fear, his Majesty's Sloop Scorpion, Commanded by the Hon. Capt. Tollemach, with a large Transport ship. These vessels have likewise been at Bermuda, and we hear that at both places they dismantled some Forts. His Excellency Governor Martin of North Carolina is on board the Scorpion.

Remarks, &c.

First part Light Breezs. & Clear Middle & latter Fresh Gales & Squally at 3 AM Carried away the Jibb Stay and Halliards, Split the Jibb. Reer'd new Stay & Halliards bent the new Jibb Handed Fore and Mizn. Topsails at 5 Split Maintopsl part of which blew away. Bent another. Close Reeft it down T. G. Yards and Masts at 12 set the Mainsail and lay too Transport in Company

---

Strong Gales and hazey with a great at 2 AM Rolled away the Driver Boom ½ past 4 Wore fir'd a six pounder p. Signal to Transport at 5 set Fore Sl. & Mizen latter Mode. set Topsails and up Top Gallt. masts, in Company as before.

First part Fresh Gales and Cloudy Middle and latter Mode. & Cloudy at 7 AM out 1st Reefs, at 8 Exercis'd Great Guns and Small Arms. Fir'd five 6 Pounders at a mark Transport in Company.

Light Breezs. & Cloudy at 2 PM bent a New Foresail Empd. Repairing the Jibb in Company as before.

Mode. & Clear, at 10 AM Lost a Log and 2 Lines, in Compy. as before.

First and Middle parts Fresh Breezs. & Squally with Rain, latter Mode. & fair at 3 PM in 1st Rfs. at 9 Sounded 50 fathm. no Ground brot too Mn. Topsl. to the Mast at 5 AM made Sail Transport in Compy.

First part Mode. & Cloudy Middle & latter Fresh Breezs. & Cloudy at 4 PM saw the Island of Bermuda W½N 6 or 7 Leags. at 10 Fir'd two Musquets pr: signal to the Transport at 3 AM fir'd 2 Guns as a Signal for a Pilot ½ past 10 Pilot came onboard Kd. brot. too & made Sail Occasly.

Fresh Breezs. and Cloudy W. at 1 PM came too with the Bt. Br. in 7 fam. in St. Georges Harbour as did the Transport Veer'd to ½ a Cable at 4 Veer'd away & Moor'd abreast of the Town. Church No. a Cables length.

On Wednesday last the Scorpions Long Boat took off this Bar, the sloop Thomas and Stafford, Solomon Gibbes, master, the property of Elias Young, of Bermuda bound here, in Ballast from St. Christopher, and the sloop Hetty, Jacob Milligan master, the property of Messrs Crouch and Grey, and James and Neilson, of this Town, bound here from Jamaica and about 60 Hogshead of rum. Both vessels were regularly cleared. There are at present in the Road, the Tamer, Thornbrough, of 20 guns, the Scorpion, Capt. Tollemache, of 14, the Cherokee, Capt. Ferguson, of 8, a transport ship, the two sloops above mentioned, and two Schooners, one of which has some swivels."

INDEX

Alderton, 14.
American provinces, 3.

Bermuda, 22(2), 23(2).
Boston, 6, 8, 11, 13, 22.
Boston Harbour, 12, 13, 14, 15, 16, 17.
Boston Lighthouse, 12.
British Public Records Office, 3.

Cambridge River, 14, 15, 16.
Campbell, Lord William, Governor of South Carolina 3(3).
Cancer, H. M. S., 17.
Cape Cod, 21.
Cape Fear, 6, 8(3), 9, 21, 22(2).
Cape Hatteras, 8.
Castle William, 12, 13, 16.
Charles Town, Mass., 15, 16, 17.
Charles Town, S. C., 8.
Charles Town (S. C.) Bar, 6, 7. 18(2), 20.
Charles Town (S. C.) Lighthouse, 7.
Cherokee, H. M. S., 23.
Colonial Records of North Carolina, The, 8.
Charles Town (S. C.) Harbour, 6.
Crouch and Grey, 23.

Dartmouth, Lord, 8.
Drew, James, 15.

Eames, Robert, 17.
Edwards, Isaac, 7.
Ellis, Richard, 7.
England, 3, 8(2).
Escott, William, 9.

Falcon, H. M. S., 13.
Ferguson, Capt., 22.
Fort Johnson, 6.
Fort Johnston (N. C.), 8.

Gibbes, Solomon, 23.
Glasgow, H. M. S., 11.
Graves, Vice-Admiral, 13(2).

Great Britain, 3.
Grey, Crouch and, 23.

Herron, Andrew, 7.
Hetty (sloop), 23.
Hobcaw, 7.

Jamaica, 23.
James and Neilson, 23.

Kings Fisher, H. M. S., 17.

Laws, John, 7.
London, 13.
Londonderry, 19.
Long Wharf, 13, 16.

Madeira, 3.
Martin, Josiah, Governor of North Carolina, 8, 22.
McGinnes, Felix, 7.
Merlin, H. M. S., 13, 17.
Milford Haven, 21.
Milligan, Jacob, 23.
Mortimer, George, 15.

Nantasket, 17.
Nantasket Bay, 13.
Nantasket Road, 16, 17.
Nantucket, 17.
Nantucket Shoals, 10.
New Providence, 9.
Newry, 11.
Neilson, James and, 23.
North America, 22.
North Carolina, 8, 22; *The Colonial Records of*, 8.

Oakes, James, 7.
Oliver, Vere L., 8.

Pallaser, 17.
Payler, George, 15.
Payne, Joshua, 7.

Philadelphia, 9, 11.
Piscataway, 11.
Preston, H. M. S., 13, 17.

Rebecca (brig.), 3.
Rebellion Road, 6, 7.
Rhode Island, 19.
Rum, 7, 23.
Ryan, James, 13.

Sanders, Capt., 3.
Sandwich Packet, 8.
Schaw, Alexander, 8.
Schaw, Jen., 8.
Somerset, H. M. S., 13, 17(2).
Smallshanks, William, 15.
South-Carolina and American General Gazette, The, 6.
South-Carolina Gazette; And Country Journal, The, 3, 6, 22.
Sr. Cruze, 21.

St. Christophers, 8, 23.
St. David's Head, 22.
St. George's Bank, Mass., 10(3), 16
St. George's Harbour, Bermuda, 22, 23.
St. George's Shoals, Mass., 10(2).
Sullivan's Island, 6.
Sunninghill, England, 8.

Tamer, H. M. S., 23.
Thomas and Stafford (sloop), 23.
Thornbrough, H. M. S., 23.
Tobago, 11.
Tompkins, William, 7.

Watts, William, 7.
West Indies, 22.
Whitmore Lodge, 8.
Wilmington, N. C., 8.

Young, Elias, 22.

Printed by Libri Plureos GmbH in Hamburg, Germany